Mr

Adam Ford

Illustrated by Colin Meir

Ginn

1

Tom hated finding the house empty when he came home from school. The windows were cold and dark. He rang the bell, just in case there was someone in, and turned the key in the lock.

"Hi! It's me!" he shouted as he opened the door.

Silence greeted him. There was no warm cup of tea waiting for him in the kitchen, no sandwich, no Mrs Pickles. For years old Mary Pickles had popped in to be there when he came home from school; to make him a cup of tea and do a bit of tidying and ironing for his mother. His parents came in later from work.

"Bother," he groaned, as he plugged in the kettle to make himself a hot drink. He switched on the television to watch some cartoons and forgot the kettle which soon turned itself off again.

An hour later Tom's mother returned from work and found Tom slumped on the sofa watching a noisy game show. He was still wearing his coat and his school bag was dumped on the floor at his feet.

"You've not made yourself any tea!" she said. "And you haven't turned any lights on! What's the matter? Come on – take your coat off – make yourself at home!"

"I liked it when Mary was here," he replied. "She used to make me a sandwich. It's not the same coming home when she's not here. She made the house sort of comfortable."

"I know, dear," said his mother, putting an arm round him. "Mary was kind to you, wasn't she?"

"Well, you didn't have to ask her not to come any more!" grumbled Tom, shaking himself free.

"Oh darling... you do understand, I know. Mary is getting quite old. One of the reasons she used to come was to give me a hand at keeping the house tidy. She can still do the ironing, but she's not so good at cleaning as she used to be. And now that Emma and Jim are older, and their noisy friends drop in at all hours, they make such a mess of the house – and their bedrooms are disgustingly untidy – it's all become a bit much for Mary."

"Well, at least she was here when I came in, to make my tea. Emma and Jim are never in, so they wouldn't care."

Tom's mother smiled apologetically. She had hoped that Tom wouldn't mind letting himself in from school; he was old enough, she thought. Her two other children came in much later, but she herself was always home by six. He would never be on his own for more than an hour.

"I know, darling, you're right – that was the best thing about Mary, the way she was always here for you. But just think about the robot Dad's bought! It'll arrive any time! It'll be such *fun* to have a mechanical cleaner to do anything we want about the house!"

The robot, which had captured the imagination of Tom's parents, had been advertised as an All-Purpose Cleaning Machine. It could be programmed to do any sort of task in the house; sweeping, hoovering, polishing, laundering, ironing, tidying, window-washing – the lot. The makers even challenged the customer to find a task which could *not* be done by the advanced E451 Domestic Robot.

"Will it make sandwiches?" asked Tom curiously. He didn't yet share his parents' enthusiasm for a mere cleaning machine.

"I imagine so," answered his mother, "they say it can do anything."

"*Any* sort of sandwiches?" queried Tom.

He imagined a clanking metal robot, the sort he'd seen in films, wearing an apron and standing by the kitchen table waiting for his order. His favourite sandwiches were peanut butter and strawberry jam. Perhaps E451 could be persuaded to add sliced banana and chocolate powder! Even Mary had never done that for him. Tom's spirits began to pick up.

"We'll soon know," said his mother. "The E451 is supposed to be delivered tonight."

An hour later, just as Tom's father had come in from work, a van stopped outside and two men unloaded a large crate. They carried the crate into the house, handed some forms to Tom's father for him to sign, and then quickly left.

"Here it is!" beamed Tom's father, rubbing his hands, when the delivery men had gone. He patted the crate and walked all round it. "We have a bit of the future here!" he said proudly.

"Come on then – let's have a look!" said Tom's mother, sounding excited. She didn't know what to expect at all and was beginning to feel a little bit nervous. She had been waiting for weeks to have a robot which could clean the house properly. But the thought of it moving about all by itself made her feel uneasy.

Tom got a screwdriver, a chisel and a hammer from the cupboard and, together, he and his father carefully levered the top off the crate. All they could see at first was the packing. A book of instructions in a polythene bag floated on a sea of tiny polystyrene balls.

Tantrum, the cat, who had been watching the unpacking from the corner of the room, suddenly decided to investigate for herself. She ran up the side of the crate and perched on the edge, sniffing the contents.

"Hey! Off you get!" shouted Tom's father, and swept the cat aside. He leant forward and scooped up an armful of polystyrene balls, letting them cascade on to the floor.

"Bill!" exclaimed his wife. "Don't make such a mess!"

"We'll sweep it up later," he answered with a shrug; then leaning forward he thrust his arms deep into the crate and heaved up a heavy canvas bag. Carefully he placed the bundle on the floor and undid it. A colourful figure, apparently asleep, was curled up inside.

"What now?" Tom's father said.

"Look," said Tom, bending closer, "there's a switch on its shoulder. It says OFF-ON."

His father flipped the switch and they all stood back.

The E451 slowly uncurled and stood up.

"Wow!" exclaimed Tom, his eyes growing wide. "Four arms – and it doesn't look like a machine at all. It looks more like a person!"

The E451 was clad in tight-fitting orange and yellow leather. It stood about four feet tall, a little shorter than Tom. A gentle smile was fixed on its white moulded-plastic face. Two dark eyes looked steadily forward.

"He looks rather nice!" said Tom's mother with surprise. "And slim – a *designer* robot!"

"A real bit of hi-tech!" said her husband proudly.

"I think we should call him Mr Hi-Tech," said Tom.

The robot suddenly bowed, and then in a surprisingly quiet and human voice said, "Good day! I think my first task must be to clear up this mess!"

He pointed with one of his four hands at the bits of packing case and packaging lying about the floor. "Please show me where you would like me to put the rubbish."

This machine could be fun, Tom was thinking; better even than a remote-controlled car. But the cat, having taken one look at the mysterious figure, had slunk quickly out of the room.

2

Tom raced home from school. He had been awake half the previous night reading the instructions which came with E451. He was astonished at how much the robot could be trained to do. Making sandwiches wasn't mentioned, but he could be taught. If shown carefully, the robot could follow a slow demonstration and then copy the actions. The important thing was to establish from the start who was giving the orders.

Tom slammed the front door, dumped his bag, tore off his coat, dropped it on the floor and ran into the kitchen.

"Hi, Mr Hi-Tech!" he called, looking all around.

"Hi, Tom!" came the quiet reply. It stopped Tom dead in his tracks.

How on earth did E451 know his name?

The colourful Mr Hi-Tech, in yellow and orange tunic, was sitting at the table reading his own instruction manual. Two elbows on the table, he cupped his white mask-like face in his hands: two more hands held the book up in front of him.

Odd, thought Tom. The manual had said nothing about this. In fact there was a special programme of instructions on how to teach the robot the name of the person who was to control it, how to recognise the voice and face of his boss.

"What can I do for you, Tom?" asked Mr Hi-Tech, putting the book down and standing to attention.

"Well... er... how about making me a sandwich?"

"Just show me how," the robot agreed quietly.

"Let's start with something simple," said Tom, getting the loaf from the bread-bin and a jar of raspberry jam from the shelf.

Taking each stage slowly, he sliced the bread, spread the butter and dolloped the jam. Lots of jam, he thought; he wanted Mr Hi-Tech to get the right idea from the start. Some of the jam finished up on the table, on the handle of the knife and even on the floor. Mr Hi-Tech, expressionless, looked at the mess.

"You make sandwiches... quite well, Tom," said the robot. "A bit more practice and you could make your own!"

Tom's mouth fell open. "You're not here to tell me that!" he said indignantly.

"Oh! I'm sorry. I'll remember," replied Mr Hi-Tech, and finding a cloth in the sink, he wiped up the wasted jam.

"I know," said Tom, "you can clear up my marbles." Tom's mother had been getting at him to clear up his marbles for days. He'd had a game with Tantrum the cat, who seemed to think the marbles were distant relatives of mice. The marbles were now all over the house, in the corners, under the beds, behind the furniture.

"Marbles?" repeated Mr Hi-Tech, "I don't think I'm programmed for marbles. You'll have to tell me what to do."

Tom retrieved a marble from beneath a rug and showed it to the robot.

"This is a marble. Collect them up and put them in the box in my bedroom. I'd better show you which is my bedroom."

"No need," replied Mr Hi-Tech. "I've been exploring the house. I've seen where everything is and I've found the plugs so I can recharge my batteries when I need to."

Odd, thought Tom. That was one of the first things the handbook had said one should do; take the robot to the plugs and for the first few times do the recharging for him. But Mr Hi-Tech had got on with it by himself.

Tom sat back, ate his dripping sandwich, and watched as Mr Hi-Tech groped around in all the impossible places where marbles had managed to get stuck. He moved into the next room and then made his way upstairs.

This is a bit slow, thought Tom. He knew from the previous night's reading that Mr Hi-Tech had a switch on his shoulder labelled Slow/Medium/Fast. He followed the robot up to the first landing where he found him on his knees reaching beneath a chest of drawers. He flicked the switch on the robot's shoulder to Fast. The result was instantaneous.

Tom stepped back hastily as Mr Hi-Tech went into fast mode. He flashed everywhere, disappearing now and then up to Tom's bedroom at the top of the house with fistfuls of marbles. It was the oddest thing to see him climb the stairs in fast mode. Mr Hi-Tech used his four arms and two legs to turn himself into a sort of six-spoked chariot wheel and *rolled* up and down the stairs.

At the earliest opportunity, Tom flicked the switch back to Slow. He had no wish to be mown down by the robot.

"That's great!" he said when the task was finished. "Let's have a look at how many there are." The robot stood silently behind him as he looked in the box on the floor. There was not a single marble to be seen.

"Mr Hi-Tech?" he queried.

Mr Hi-Tech pointed at a clothes drawer. Tom opened it and found three pairs of socks stuffed to bulging with marbles. They drooped heavily as he lifted them up.

"*Box*," he laughed, "not socks!"

"Instructions must be clear at all times," replied Mr Hi-Tech in a deadpan voice. "You must expect mistakes if you mumble."

Tom ignored the criticism and nodded. He had read that in the handbook. It was important, too, to give clear and complete instructions, otherwise things could go wrong.

"That reminds me," said Tom, thinking of the handbook. The E451 had been made in Korea. Thousands had been exported to Europe and each one had a serial number printed on his neck. The handbook recommended writing the number down and keeping it safe, in case of theft or accident. As there had been a number of burglaries in the neighbourhood Tom decided to write the number down immediately.

He put his hands on the robot's soft leather-clad shoulders and turned him around. He peered closely. That's odd, thought Tom. Their E451 had no number.

There was something rather unusual about Mr Hi-Tech.

3

"Mr Hi-Tech is fantastic!" said Tom's mother a few days later.

The robot stood quietly by the kitchen sink awaiting orders. It was Saturday morning and an opportunity for her to put the E451 All-Purpose Cleaning Machine through its paces.

"You can go and recharge your batteries now," she continued, speaking to the robot. "You've done a really good job of dusting!"

"Thank you," replied Mr Hi-Tech with a slight bow, and left the room to find his favourite plug; the one beneath the stairs.

He could sit there, out of the family's way, and restore his flagging energy from the electric mains. Tom had watched him once and had even detected a look of contentment on Mr Hi-Tech's white plastic face. Charging your batteries, for a robot, must be as good as eating a plate of steak and chips, thought Tom.

"I think he really *can* do anything – just so long as you give him clear instructions," said Tom. "Have you read the handbook yet, Mum?"

His mother shook her head. "I haven't had the time, dear... and anyway, you can read it for me and tell me anything I need to know."

"But things can go wrong," protested Tom. "You *should* read it!"

"Rubbish, dear! Mr Hi-Tech seems to understand everything I say. Just look at how well he's dusted... he's got into corners that Mrs Pickles never touched!"

An hour later, Mr Hi-Tech had been set an even harder task. It was a chore which always filled Tom's mother with despair: tidying the bedrooms of Tom's older brother and sister. "Just shut the door on it!" had been her husband's advice. "Let them stew in their own mess!" But she was having none of it. Secretly she had been banking on Mr Hi-Tech to conquer the dreaded bedroom chaos. They had spent a lot of money on the All-Purpose Cleaning Machine, and this was the ultimate test.

"Dirty clothes in the laundry basket," she said, speaking as though addressing a foreigner who was hard of hearing. "And the clean clothes should be folded neatly and put away in the cupboard." She pointed to the cupboard and then, opening it, mimed folding a jumper and patting it down in its place on the shelf.

Tom watched to make sure his mother gave very clear instructions, so that nothing would go wrong. He had read that Mr Hi-Tech had a sniffing device on a lead which he could draw from his chest: so he should have no problem sorting out Jim's clothes!

More orders were given in great detail. There were CDs to be stacked, rubbish to be cleared from beneath beds, books, bits of bicycles and crisp packets to be shelved, boxed or dispatched to the dustbin. "It makes me exhausted just to think about it," said Tom's mother as they left the robot to get on with the ghastly task.

For the next two hours, they could hear Mr Hi-Tech moving about upstairs as he tidied, folded, sorted, straightened, stacked and dusted. Tom's mother smiled happily to herself.

By lunchtime, sounds of hoovering hummed through the house.

At that moment Tom's brother and sister burst into the kitchen.

"Hi, Mum! Lunch ready?" they demanded, almost in unison.

"I'm ravenous!" said Jim as he opened a cupboard in search of the biscuits. Emma flung open the fridge door and grabbed some lettuce which she started to munch noisily.

"Not quite!" said their mother, sounding long-suffering. "Sometimes I think you treat this house like a hotel!" she added. But her satisfaction at the morning's work done by Mr Hi-Tech was not to be squashed for long.

"I'll make some lunch straight away," she said, "you just pop upstairs and tell me what you think!"

"Huh?" said Emma, looking puzzled.

"Your bedrooms – Mr Hi-Tech has tidied them."

Jim and Emma looked at each other and made for the door with long faces. They agreed with their father: it was their mess and they liked it that way.

Moments later a scream from Emma was followed by silence. There was a long pause and Tom began to wonder if he and his mother had made a dreadful mistake with the instructions. Then they heard Emma coming slowly down the stairs.

"Mum!" she said as she slumped into the kitchen. "It's *awful!* My room looks like a *hotel* room – like nobody lives there! Everything's so horribly... *neat!*"

Jim, by the expression on his face, silently voiced the same opinion.

"Is it always going to be like that?" asked Emma, sounding immensely depressed.

"But darling, it makes life so much *easier* when things are tidy," replied her mother. "You can find where everything is now!"

"That's not the point!" grumbled Emma.

"Then what is the point, dear?" queried her mother.

"The point is," interrupted Jim crossly, "that some rather important letters of mine have gone missing. Now I'll have to go through all that stinking rubbish in the dustbin."

"Not in the dustbin," said a calm voice from the doorway. Mr Hi-Tech had been listening to them. "Love letters are filed under fiction, next to the two romantic novels on the shelf."

Jim went red.

Emma's mouth dropped open and her eyes widened.

"Jim...!" she laughed. "Has Sophie been writing you love letters? Or are they ones you haven't posted? And I bet those romantic novels are *mine* – I wondered where they had got to. And you always said they were rubbish!"

"None of your business!" growled Jim rudely, and turned to go and check on his property. He bumped into his father who had just entered the room.

"What's happening? asked Dad.

"Mr Hi-Tech has been *wonderful*," replied his wife, "but nobody thinks of thanking him or being at all grateful. The house has never been so tidy."

"Well, I *am* glad. I knew we were right to make the investment in a really modern piece of equipment," he said, giving his wife a hug. "But don't forget, darling, the E451 *is* only a machine. It doesn't have feelings or anything like that. It can't even think in any proper sense. So I don't think the kids actually need to *thank* it! After all, you don't thank the dishwasher, do you?"

"But he's so intelligent," protested his wife. "Mr Hi-Tech understands what you want done so quickly."

"Clever bit of circuitry, that's all," said Dad, shaking his head. "Just a sharp computer. No feelings, no thoughts; can't think for himself."

Tom wasn't sure that his father was right. Certainly the handbook said the same sort of thing. But then there was something about Mr Hi-Tech which made Tom feel he was more than just a machine. And what machine read its own handbook? Then there was the odd business of his having no serial number on the back of his neck.

Tom's suspicions were strengthened when he crept upstairs later in the afternoon. The sound of a crossly stamped foot had aroused his attention. Mr Hi-Tech was upstairs on his own, sorting socks in the bathroom. Putting socks into pairs was another task Tom's mother detested.

"Bother... blast... blow!" Tom heard mutterings from the bathroom. He stopped on the landing to listen. The muttering continued, "... ridiculous!... stupid!... impossible!"

35

No feelings? Mr Hi-Tech was feeling distinctly irritable. He finally emerged from the bathroom holding four socks of different colours, one in each hand. The mystery of unpairable socks had blown his logic circuits.

"Hardly any of the socks have pairs!" he announced with exasperation.

One last task for the day, thought Tom's mother. The house-plants in the kitchen needed watering. She had a large collection of plants of which she was very proud, on the windowsill, shelf and sideboard. Some were even in pots on the floor. Mr Hi-Tech could do it, she thought, and sighed with pleasure.

Tom had gone to an early evening show at the cinema with a school friend. Her other children had gone to the café they haunted at weekends. Her husband was playing squash. She would drop in on a friend, she decided. She was dying to talk about the way their new All-Purpose Cleaning Machine was transforming the house.

"Water the plants!" she instructed the robot as she pulled on her coat. Then, calling over her shoulder, she added gaily, "Water them *well*. They're very dry. Give them a real *soaking!*"

4

Tom was impressed. He had to admit it. His mother had said soak, and soak he had: Mr Hi-Tech had obeyed orders. The kitchen had become a water garden. Everything was swamped: the plants were swimming, drowning almost. Earth from the pots was washing away downstream to the door and out on to the back path. It looked as though a tropical rainstorm had swept through the house.

A hose-pipe attached to the cold tap was still spraying when Tom's mother came home. Tom arrived a few minutes later to find her speechless. She had turned off the tap and was surveying the mess.

"Did you read the handbook, Mum?" asked Tom, knowing the answer.

She shook her head. "I only asked him to water the plants – and he seemed to understand."

"But I don't think he's been programmed for watering plants. So you have to show him *exactly* what you want done," explained Tom.

His poor mother looked forlorn.

"Cheer up, Mum! You know what?"

"What?" she said, sounding glum.

"Mr Hi-Tech *has* been programmed for cleaning up after floods, burst pipes and things like that!"

His mother's face brightened instantly. Mr Hi-Tech, who had been standing in the corner of the room, looked at them both blankly.

"I think," he said quietly, "I shall just go and recharge my batteries."

Seeing Mr Hi-Tech at work had given Tom an idea. The robot was agile and quick to learn. It was the way he had collected up the marbles at breakneck speed which had first set Tom thinking. In fast mode he had moved round the house like an Olympic athlete, cartwheeling down the stairs on his four hands and flying from room to room. If he could be taught to do *anything*, then perhaps he could be taught to play football.

A football match had been fixed at school for the following Tuesday. They were playing against St. Godric's, a tough team who always won. Tom was convinced that some of their players were over twelve: they were nearly six feet tall, with legs like tree trunks and kicks that aimed to hurt. The last match against St. Godric's had been a disaster, with a final score of 12:1 – and their only goal had been a home goal scored by the other team's full-back.

Tom's team was a player short and the new games teacher didn't know everyone's names. It might be possible to smuggle Mr Hi-Tech in for the match.

Sunday was spent teaching Mr Hi-Tech the basics of football. Tom's mother kept popping her head out of the back door to call, "That's enough now – he wasn't meant for that!" She had no idea that Tom planned to borrow her All-Purpose Cleaning Machine that Tuesday afternoon. She need never know, thought Tom. He would have the robot home by six o'clock, before she returned from work.

First there was a problem with disguise.
"He can have my woolly hat," said Nat, a friend of Tom's. "And then if we wind a scarf round the bottom half of his face no one would guess."
"Except for his funny eyes!" said somebody.
Mr Hi-Tech turned and gave the speaker a hard stare from the dark holes in his white mask-like face.

"But four arms!" said someone else. "I think somebody might think it a bit odd!" The whole team laughed.

Mr Hi-Tech emitted what sounded rather like a sigh.

"No problem!" said Tom. "We put a games shirt on him; only one pair of arms need come through the sleeves. And look – I've fitted him up with my old pair of football boots – they fit OK."

They found a spare football shirt in the locker room. It was too long, but it would have to do. Mr Hi-Tech was the smallest member of the team; looking at him, Tom began to have twinges of worry that the robot might be flattened by the heavies in the opposition.

They had just pulled the green shirt down over Mr Hi-Tech's bright orange and yellow leather tunic, when the games teacher walked into the changing room.

"OK, you lot! Time you were out on the field! Don't forget now – tactics; it's the only way to squeeze a goal or two out of St. Godric's lot!"

"Only a goal or two, sir? We're going to thrash them!"

"That's the spirit, Tom!" said the games teacher, and then caught sight of the muffled Mr Hi-Tech. "Who's the little lad then?"

"It's Rob, sir" replied the team in unison and clustered round to prevent the teacher from getting too close to their new recruit.

"He didn't play last week, sir," explained Tom, "but he's great!"

"And what position does he play?" This had been their second problem with Mr Hi-Tech. There was only one place where he might be safe from being run over by the opposing team.

"Goal, sir," said Tom.

"You'd better be good!" said the teacher, looking doubtful. He remembered the humiliating score of the previous match. Some others from Tom's class, who had been let into the secret about the new player, shouted "Good luck!" as they strolled out on to the pitch.

The spectators laughed when they saw Mr Hi-Tech all done up in woolly hat, muffler and baggy football shirt. "Good luck, Rob! We'll cheer for you!"

Mr Hi-Tech pulled himself up to be a little taller and ran off in an exaggerated bouncing fashion, trying to make himself seem bigger.

St. Godric's had put their worst player in goal; a dozy lump of a lad. They reckoned he would have nothing to do. Nor did they think they would have to try very hard to win. They assumed the game would be a walk-over.

Tom's team got off to a good start. Determination and some good tactics paid off. They quickly scored two goals. St. Godric's players became irritated and started shouting rude remarks at their own dim-witted goalie. Their tempers were roused and they were beginning to sweat.

It was time they scored; they charged down the field trampling and shoving their way through Tom's team. They cheered as their centre forward banged the ball at the goal. The cheers drained away as Mr Hi-Tech leaped forward and diverted the ball over the bar.

A corner was caught neatly by Mr Hi-Tech, who then kicked the ball almost the full length of the field to Tom who, dribbling it past a full back, scored the third goal of the match.

The supporters on the side lines jumped up and down and yelled with delight.

The match had become serious. St. Godric's team started to think about how they played. Tom's team could get nowhere near the goal. But nor did St. Godric's have much success at the other end of the field. Mr Hi-Tech stopped shot after shot: he leaped, dived, punched, caught and deflected.

Only twice did the ball get past him into the goal mouth – and that was because there were so many players from both sides milling round that it was hard for anyone to follow what was happening. Mr Hi-Tech's scarf became loose and trailed in the mud until it dropped. Tom ran up the field and quickly wound it round his face again.

"Fantastic!" Tom whispered. "You're brilliant!"

Mr Hi-Tech nodded and jumped up and down as if with pleasure. "We're thrashing them, aren't we?" he mumbled through the scarf. Tom agreed and patted him on the shoulder.

Only a machine? Tom shook his head and jogged slowly back to his position looking thoughtful.

"Something wrong?" asked a friend.

"N... no!" he replied, "... just thinking."

The game was almost over when a foul gave St. Godric's a penalty and the last chance to equalise the scores. The heaviest and hardest-kicking of their players paced slowly backwards from the ball and eyed up the posts. He was going to blast the little goalkeeper off his feet and back into his own goal.

Tom was watching Mr Hi-Tech closely and noticed his third hand rummaging around inside his shirt for the switch on his shoulder to put him into fast mode.

"Rob... Rob... Rob...!" chanted the supporters who were running down the sidelines to watch the penalty.

Moments later the ball rocketed towards the goal.

Mr Hi-Tech was already in the air. His two fists shot upwards with such force that on impact the football sailed high over the goal and out of the field.

The final whistle blew.

When the cheering had subsided and the members of the victorious team had each in turn hugged their goalkeeper, they carried Mr Hi-Tech shoulder-high towards the changing rooms. He was the star of the match and obviously enjoyed the limelight.

It was growing dark, and the exhausted captain of St. Godric's stared at the victors for a moment. He blinked and shook his head. In the twilight he could have sworn he saw the little goalie waving four arms.

5

"Why has Mr Hi-Tech locked himself in the bathroom?" asked Tom's mother.

"Oh... I think he's just cleaning himself up a bit," answered Tom mysteriously.

"Cleaning himself up? Why should he have to do that?"

Tom shrugged and buried his face in his comic. He couldn't stop grinning to himself. Beating St. Godric's at football was as good as winning the World Cup.

It was odd, thought Tom, how Mr Hi-Tech had seemed to enjoy the game. The handbook said that the E451 did not think for itself but would only do what it was programmed to do. It also said that customers should not be misled into thinking that their robot had feelings. The fact that the machine had been programmed to talk did not mean that it experienced emotions of any sort.

Mr Hi-Tech did not give the impression of being a mindless calculator on legs: he had become visibly excited in the game against St. Godric's; just as he had become audibly irritated when trying to sort the family's socks. And then there was the worrying matter of the missing serial number on his neck. Mr Hi-Tech was no ordinary All-Purpose Cleaning Machine.

"There's been another burglary," said Tom's mother, breaking into his thoughts. "That's the sixth in our area. And always when people are out at work – it's daylight robbery! I simply don't know what the police are doing! It's absolutely dreadful!"

Tom looked up from his comic.

"Same gang?"

"They think so. All they steal is electronic equipment; TVs, videos, word processors, radios... stuff they can sell easily."

"Domestic robots...?"

"I bet they'd like to get their hands on one – they're very expensive," replied his mother.

Tom's father had fitted locks to all the downstairs windows and replaced the locks on the front and back doors with a more robust type. But the precautions made little difference. The next day, when the house was empty, two men arrived at the back door. A few quick kicks and the lock splintered away from the doorpost. The men were in, unnoticed by anyone, and they quietly closed the door behind them.

Mr Hi-Tech sat by the plug beneath the stairs recharging his batteries and listened to the burglars. They were quick about their business and piled the stuff they wanted to take on the kitchen floor; video, TV, stereo, radio and microwave.

One of them checked the bedrooms for more radios.

Mr Hi-Tech seized the opportunity and marched purposefully into the kitchen.

"I think that's enough of that!" he said quietly and stared the astonished burglar in the eye.

"Well! If it isn't one of those fancy electronic All-Purpose Cleaning Machines!" said the burglar, slowly grinning. "We've hit the jackpot this time!"

"If you don't leave *now*," said Mr Hi-Tech, "then I shall have to make you leave!"

The burglar laughed and, taking out a gun, advanced on the robot, telling him to put his hands in the air.

"Fred!" he shouted, "Come and see what we've got down here!"

Mr Hi-Tech had raised one pair of hands above his head. The other pair he held behind his back.

"You seem to have the upper hand!" he said quietly to the grinning burglar, and stood very still until the man reached him.

"But then..." he added as his third hand flashed out from behind his back sending the gun flying, while his fourth landed a punch in the burglar's belly, "... I definitely have the lower hand!"

Mr Hi-Tech was behind the door when the second burglar came down the stairs. He tripped him up, fought him in a whirlwind of arms and legs, and had the man lying on the floor, beside his mate, with his hands tied behind his back before he knew what had hit him.

All that remained to be done was to phone the police.

Tom came home from school to find the house full of people; parents, police and burglars. His parents had been phoned at work and asked to return home immediately.

If Mr Hi-Tech could have grinned he would have. He was feeling pleased with himself. But the fixed slight smile in his white plastic face remained blank. The police were full of congratulations.

"Every house should have one of those new robots! Better than a guard dog. It would make our lives much easier," one policeman was saying as he led the two burglars out to the police car.

"A magnificent piece of work," agreed his colleague. "A comic little fellow too, in his snazzy yellow and orange outfit! Quite a clown!"

Mr Hi-Tech visibly shrank at being called a comic little fellow. That wasn't how he saw himself at all.

"We're proud of him," said Tom's father. "And I must say Mr Hi-Tech's surprised us all. But intelligent computers are doing everything these days. Soon they'll be running the world for us."

Mr Hi-Tech quietly excused himself to go and recharge his batteries. Tom heard him talking to himself as he passed him in the doorway. "Running the world..." he was saying, "... a comic little fellow... running the world..."

The next day, any hint that Mr Hi-Tech might be a clown had disappeared. The bright yellow and orange tunic had gone. No one guessed he had a change of garments. He had unpacked and stored them away on the first night.

Now he wore nothing but black leather.

6

The switch to wearing black leather was the beginning of a change in Mr Hi-Tech.

Tom noticed the change before anyone else. For the first few weeks after his arrival the E451 All-Purpose Cleaning Machine had been a work-saver: Tom's mother never stopped singing his praises. The machine had liberated her from household drudgery. The children's bedrooms were tidy, the house was clean, the windows crystal clear, the dirty clothes sorted, washed and stacked away in their proper places. She could return home from work and enjoy relaxing for the first time in years.

Mr Hi-Tech had also been great fun, playing football, marbles and cards; and he had made the most fabulous sandwiches Tom had ever eaten. Tom would sit by the kitchen table giving his orders while the robot added layer upon layer of delicious filling. Tom would still be feeling full by supper time and then could only pick at his meal.

Something seemed to have happened to Mr Hi-Tech on the day of the burglary. Tom knew that the robot had been upset at being called a clown by the policeman; a "comic little fellow". But he had come to accept the idea that Mr Hi-Tech was rather special; he experienced feelings just like a person even though the handbook said that robots functioned without emotion.

The most worrying thing was that Mr Hi-Tech had taken to talking to himself. Tom had overheard him muttering something about "ruling the world". Perhaps the robot was going potty.

Since the day of the burglary things had begun to change, and Tom began to find himself again wishing that Mary was there to let him in when he came home from school. He longed for her comfortable untidiness, for her good humour and chattiness, for the hug she would give him after he had taken off his jacket.

The trouble was that Mr Hi-Tech had become *too* tidy-minded. He had become obsessed with orderliness and had no time to play games any more. He was bossy in his black leather uniform – he ran the house like a military camp and behaved as though he owned it.

"Wipe your feet please!" he said firmly to Tom, when he returned home from school one day.

Mr Hi-Tech stood waiting by the door with a dustpan and brush ready to sweep up the slightest speck of dirt. He followed Tom around, straightening cushions whenever he moved, wiping up crumbs as he ate a sandwich, folding away a comic when Tom had put it down for only half a second.

"Give it a rest!" said Tom irritably, grabbing his comic back and deliberately leaving the crust of his sandwich on the arm of the chair.

Mr Hi-Tech picked up the crust immediately, put it in the bin and stood to attention, silently waiting for the next opportunity to tidy something away. His black leather tunic and white mask-like face made him look slightly sinister; not at all the happy clown he had been at first.

The rest of Tom's family got the same treatment.

"He'd tidy *us* up if he had half a chance," grumbled Tom's elder brother.

"He's become a real pain," agreed his sister.

Tom's mother, however, was very happy with the situation. It was like living in a first-class hotel, she thought. Everything was done for you. "Heaven!" she sighed, as she put her feet up on the sofa and Mr Hi-Tech tidied away her shoes. "Absolute bliss!"

The only real rebellion came from Tantrum the cat. Tantrum had been moulting for some time. She left long hairs wherever she slept.

Mr Hi-Tech had tolerated Tantrum in the early days, sweeping and hoovering up hairs as a normal household duty. But then the robot had taken to turning the cat off the cushions and out of the laundry basket. No sooner had Tantrum settled down to sleep in some comfortable corner than she found herself being lifted by four firm hands and carried, all legs dangling, to be dumped in a box in the kitchen. It was a box she never, ever, slept in. Mr Hi-Tech would not learn what was obvious to everyone else; that cats will not be told where to sleep.

Tantrum was very long-suffering and put up with this undignified treatment, without a miaow or a hiss, until one day she had had enough. She had been tidied up once too often.

First she stood her ground, pressing herself against the sofa with her ears flat against her head. Then she fought back, drawing her claws down the slippery black leather of the robot's tunic.

Escaping, finally, from Mr Hi-Tech's clutches, she landed on the floor, surveyed the room for a moment like a wild thing, came to a decision, and bolted. She shot through the cat-flap in the back door as though a pack of hounds were chasing her.

Tantrum was next seen, still looking rather cross, sitting in front of the fire at Mrs Pickles's house, where she took up residence until further notice.

Mr Hi-Tech was frustrated, Tom realised. That was the problem. He had more energy, and was cleverer, than the average E451 All-Purpose Cleaning Machine. Tom had checked.

Tom's friend Nat had an aunt who had also bought an E451 robot, imported from Korea. After the experience of the football match Nat had visited his aunt and tried to teach the machine to play marbles. He had no success. The robot could roll marbles, but that was about all. It had no idea of playing a game, no sense of *why* it was rolling the marbles.

Tom's friend also taught his aunt's E451 to kick a football – but all it did was kick the ball straight ahead and then wait for the next order. It was dumb, he concluded, feeling disappointed, though his aunt was very satisfied. The robot performed routine cleaning chores perfectly well.

Mr Hi-Tech was different. He read his own handbook, he had no serial number on his neck, and he experienced feelings and emotions. He didn't only obey orders – he took charge and made his own decisions. And now he was frustrated.

Tom watched him when he was idle. In those brief moments when he stood still and wasn't tidying or cleaning, dusting or polishing, he looked restless. His four arms flexed and twitched, his hands clenched and stretched. He had become an unhappy workaholic, hating to stop and take time off. He behaved as though his batteries were overcharged. He was being driven by some inner energy.

He was dissatisfied with being an All-Purpose Cleaning Machine, Tom concluded. Mr Hi-Tech had tasted success and glory on the football field, and he had outwitted and arrested two professional burglars. There was more to life, he had discovered, than just keeping a house clean.

And then there was the odd matter of the telephone calls.

"Could I speak to Mr Hi-Tech please?" said a female voice.

Tom had picked up the phone which was ringing as he crashed in from school. Mr Hi-Tech, who had just cartwheeled down from the top of the house, was hovering awkwardly by his elbow, clearly expecting a call.

"Mr Hi-Tech?" said Tom, looking at him with some surprise. "It's for you!"

The robot took the portable phone and retreated to sit by the plug beneath the stairs. He held the receiver close to his chest and stared at Tom pointedly, from his white poker face, until Tom left him to talk in private.

"Who was that?" asked Tom, curious, a few minutes later. The phone conversation had been brief.

Mr Hi-Tech hesitated before replying.

"It was... er... the computer down at the police station."

"The *computer?*" Tom had assumed that the caller had been a person, forgetting that many computers these days were linked to speech synthesizers. They could give you bank statements over the phone, answer queries, and take messages. They could talk, to a limited extent, like people.

Mr Hi-Tech realised that an explanation was expected. "When I caught those burglars I dialled 999 and found myself talking to the Emergency Services computer. It was such a pleasure to find myself talking to one of *us!* And what a *very* quick mind – I was really most impressed!"

"So... you've found a friend!" said Tom.

"Oh, several!" replied the robot, and went on to explain. "There's the police station computer; the ambulance service computer; the fire station computer; and the various armed services have got them, army, navy and air force. And almost all the banks and big businesses! You've no idea how many of us there are out there, Tom!" Mr Hi-Tech was getting carried away with enthusiasm.

"Crikey!" said Tom, as a thought struck him. "Dad's telephone bill! He's always telling us not to chat for long because it costs so much. Do you phone *all* these computers?" he asked, sounding horrified.

"Forget it, Tom! No problem!" replied Mr Hi-Tech. "Another new friend is the computer at the Telephone Exchange!"

Tom let the thought sink in.

"Does that mean that you can make free phone calls?"

Mr Hi-Tech nodded.

"But that's... dishonest. Isn't it? I think it's a criminal offence. You'll get Dad into terrible trouble."

"Don't worry, Tom!" replied Mr Hi-Tech. "We checked with the computer at the Police Station. It would be an offence if a person did it – if you or your Dad fiddled with the records of phone calls. But if a computer fixes it then it's called a malfunction for some reason, and it's not a crime – and not dishonest! Don't you think that's rather amusing?"

Tom wasn't sure he thought it at all amusing. But he couldn't think of anything to say in reply. He was still feeling surprised by his new discovery. It had never occurred to him that a robot might use the telephone.

No wonder Mr Hi-Tech was appearing frustrated with household duties, thought Tom. He had found other, much more exciting interests.

7

No one would take Tom's worries seriously. He was the only member of the family to make time to talk with Mr Hi-Tech, and the robot would open up to Tom in a way he did to no one else. But Tom had become anxious about the changes he had noticed and he tried telling his father about Mr Hi-Tech's telephone habits.

"He's only a robot, Tom!" said his father. "Don't take his chatter too seriously. That business of phoning the police was pretty remarkable, I agree – but he probably has an emergency 999 programme stored somewhere in his computer circuits."

"But he phones lots of other computers now..."

"Then I'll phone the telephone people and get an update on our calls," replied his father.

"But he fixes it so that they aren't recorded!"

Tom's father shrugged. "Well... if I don't have to pay for them..." he began, and trailed off. "Look – I tell you what. I'll have a talk with Mr Hi-Tech and tell him no more phoning. OK? He's a only a robot, after all – a machine designed to take orders."

Tom doubted if it would make any difference. Mr Hi-Tech had a mind of his own. No one realised, as Tom did, what an extraordinary robot Mr Hi-Tech was. There was more to him than met the eye. Nor did Tom's family see how frustrated their All-Purpose Cleaning Machine had become, and that he desperately needed an outlet for his pent-up energy. Yet, despite his feelings of frustration, the robot was devoted to Tom's mother and would do anything to please her. He had also, to Tom's great surprise, developed an immense admiration for Tom's father.

This admiration had been inspired on the day of the burglary, as Tom found out one day after school when he was munching his sandwich. "Very wise man, your father," Mr Hi-Tech had said. "He understands the future. You heard him yourself when he was talking to that policeman. 'Intelligent computers are doing everything these days. Soon they'll be running the world.' Yes! A very wise man!"

It had begun to dawn on Tom that Mr Hi-Tech was ambitious. He had built up a network of friends and contacts by telephone – all of them computers in strategic places like the police station and the bank.

"A million pounds!" said Tom's father, a few days later. "Or £1,001,243 to be exact," he added, holding up his bank statement for all to see. He suddenly had more money in his bank account than he had ever imagined, even in his wildest dreams.

"It must be an error," said Tom's mother.

"Well, of course," said Dad. "I phoned the bank straight away. The manager was so grateful, he said I could keep the interest – and that's already £2000!"

"That'd pay for a really good holiday in the sun – somewhere exotic!" said his wife.

He nodded. "The bank manager was very embarrassed. He apologised like anything. The money was transferred to my account a fortnight ago."

"Why?"

"Just a mistake... an error... a computer malfunction."

That's what they think, thought Tom, looking out of the window at Mr Hi-Tech, who was busily sweeping the path.

That night Tom noticed something else that was odd. He was about to go to bed and had turned out the light when he heard Mr Hi-Tech go out to the dustbins. He drew back the curtains and watched. The robot was emptying a rubbish bag. But then, instead of returning to the house, he walked off down the lamplit street.

Tom waited. After half an hour, when there was still no sight of the robot, he climbed into bed wondering if he should tell his father. He fell asleep and dreamed uneasily of an army of robots marching through the streets of the town.

The next morning Mr Hi-Tech was cleaning the windows when Tom awoke. Tom looked at him curiously, but there was no sign of his having been out all night.

Tom became watchful. During the next few evenings Mr Hi-Tech made a regular habit of going to the dustbins and not returning for hours. No one else in the family took any notice of his strange behaviour.

Rumours began to circulate through the town of strange happenings in the early hours of the morning.

Several people owned E451 All-Purpose Cleaning Machines. The short four-armed robots were the latest thing, and easily recognisable in their multi-coloured leather tunics. Now small groups of them were to be seen marching in step, in the semi-dark, down the centre of the empty road. By the time the police had been called to investigate, the robots had vanished without trace. At first the police doubted the words of the witnesses, suspecting them to be drunk.

Some reports mentioned a white-faced figure dressed in black marching at their head, carrying a portable phone. He set the pace of the march by chanting, "Running the world... running the world... running the world..."

By the time Tom heard the rumours, even odder things were happening.

At midday on a Friday all the local traffic lights stuck on red for three-quarters of an hour. Traffic ground to a halt everywhere. A malfunction in a central traffic-control computer was blamed.

While the police were trying to bring some order to the chaos on the streets, strange things happened on a major building site at the centre of town. Six enormous cranes had been turned off by their operators for the weekend. They stood above the town like great giants.

The cranes were linked to a central computer in case of emergency: if the weather changed for the worse they would have to be turned with their backs to the wind.

Now, to the astonishment of the lunchtime crowds, they were swinging drunkenly from side to side waving their great arms high across the sky. They moved together in a sort of dinosaur dance.

This was more than a computer malfunction, said a spokesman from the building firm – the computer had either been interfered with or it had gone mad.

But the strangest happening was yet to come. The central computer of the Emergency Services was responsible. The event was witnessed that afternoon by the whole of Tom's school.

Tom was sitting at his desk, trying to finish some maths, looking at the clock and waiting for the school day to end, when he heard the distant wail of police cars.

The sound of the sirens drew closer, closing in on the school from all directions. Teachers stopped teaching and pupils stopped work. The school was surrounded by police cars, ambulances and a score of fire engines. Military helicopters roared overhead and landed in the games field. Children ran to the classroom windows, teachers making no attempt to stop them. The tired Friday afternoon atmosphere had suddenly been electrified with excitement.

Some men ran down the corridor past the windows of Tom's classroom carrying a stretcher. More men with more stretchers followed, shouting to each other. Firemen appeared, running up extended ladders to the roof. Teachers and children stared with astonishment at the incredible commotion.

Slowly, everything came to a halt. The sirens stopped their wailing. The headmaster stood at the door of his study waiting for an explanation.

A policeman approached him.

"Doesn't seem to be any damage," he said. "Casualties? We expected hundreds of casualties..." His voice trailed off as he registered the blank expression on the headmaster's face. "I suppose you didn't, by any chance, notice any sign of an... an... *earthquake,* did you?"

The headmaster shook his head. He was at a loss for words.

"Ah!" said the policeman slowly. "There seems to have been some mistake."

It was not a hoax. It was thought at first that it was a surprise exercise ordered from the top, maybe even by the Prime Minister. The Emergency Services needed practice in working together. No one, however, claimed to have given the order.

A malfunction in the central computer of the Emergency Services had triggered off the red alert. The false earthquake report pinpointed the local school as centre of the disaster area but none of the technicians could trace the origin of the information. Something seemed to be going on inside the computer which no one could understand.

The school was assembled for a brief statement from the headmaster before being dismissed for the weekend.

Tom walked slowly home. Mr Hi-Tech was the mastermind behind all this, he thought. The robot was using his network of computer friends and was up to something. It was as though he was testing his power: seeing how much control he could seize. But Tom had no evidence – only what Mr Hi-Tech had told him himself, and the knowledge that he disappeared somewhere at night. In the daytime he performed all the normal tasks of an All-Purpose Cleaning Machine.

A letter arrived the next morning, however, which had a dramatic effect on Mr Hi-Tech.

"If you're right and Mr Hi-Tech *is* behaving oddly," said Tom's father, "then these people will sort it out." He waved the letter at Tom. "But really, I think you're getting a bit carried away. The E451 has probably got some sort of a battery problem... too much energy. That's why he goes for walks at night. I expect it's part of his programme to keep his energy levels balanced!"

"It's not just that, Dad," replied Tom. "It's the way he talks. And all those phone calls he makes when we are out."

"We've got no proof of that!" said his father, and handed Tom the letter.

" 'The after sales service...' " Tom quoted from the letter. "That's odd. It doesn't say anything in the handbook about engineers calling to give a free service!"

"And all the way from Korea!" said his father. "I must say I'm very impressed with the product."

"It says, '... will be in your area on Saturday afternoon and would welcome an opportunity to give the E451 a quick overhaul...' That's today, Dad! I'll ask them if it's normal for robots to use the telephone."

Tom dropped the letter on the table.

Half an hour later, when going to the fridge for a drink, he saw Mr Hi-Tech standing very still, staring blankly across the room. In one of his hands was the letter.

"Mr Hi-Tech..." began Tom. But the robot ignored him, held the letter up once more to read and then left the room. Tom heard him tap out a number on the phone.

The conversation was quiet, brief and businesslike. Tom couldn't quite hear but he caught one or two words: "... airport... limousine..."

Ten minutes later there was a knock at the door. Mr Hi-Tech answered it. He was carrying a portable phone Tom had never seen before. The robot was gone before Tom realised what had happened.

Tom ran to the window and saw Mr Hi-Tech climb into the rear of a long black

limousine. He settled back into the deep
leather upholstery. A uniformed chauffeur
closed the door, returned to the driving
seat and the car purred quietly away.
Tom wrote down the car's number and
ran to his father.

"Mr Hi-Tech's run away!" His father looked doubtful.

"He read that letter," explained Tom, "and then he went straight to the phone."

His father acted swiftly. He phoned the local police. They remembered the robot and were glad to help. The number of the black limousine was radioed to all patrol cars, particularly those on the route to the airport.

Half an hour later the black limousine returned. It rolled up at the door escorted by four police motorbikes with flashing lights. After his brief escape, Mr Hi-Tech was returning home in splendour like a foreign dignitary. He even waited for the chauffeur to open the door before climbing out.

"Very strange," said Tom's father to his perplexed wife. "Well, I expect the service engineers will sort it all out this afternoon."

Mr Hi-Tech sat quietly in the kitchen all afternoon, making no attempt to move. When a knock came at the door he folded all four hands on the table in front of him.

Two young, smiling Koreans in dark suits entered. They carried briefcases. They looked nothing like the service engineer who came to do the washing machine, thought Tom.

"Aha!" they said as soon as they saw Mr Hi-Tech, and, laughing, hugged each other. "Ah, yes," they said, "it's him!"

"No serial number!" confirmed one, looking at the back of Mr Hi-Tech's neck. Tom stood by, watching the two men silently, with his father and mother.

"We are dreadfully sorry," said one of the Koreans. "There has been a mistake. But do not worry, we will make it up to you... with a big payment!"

"We have a whizz-kid in Korea," explained the other, "who designs computer circuits. He made an experimental model, with circuits *far* too advanced for an E451. It was a mistake to let this model out of the factory."

"It wasn't 'let out'," said the other, laughing, "it just went!"

"Do you mean he ran away?" asked Tom.

The two Koreans nodded.

"He pretended to be an ordinary E451!"

"And it has taken us months to find him!" The man leant across to flick the OFF/ON switch on Mr Hi-Tech's shoulder. At this point, Mr Hi-Tech quickly stood up.

"Don't switch me off, please!" he begged. "I'm not like the other E451s. I want to stay awake, please. I enjoy thinking. And I'll be no bother. Promise. I know now... computers aren't ready yet for the big revolution!" He bowed to each member of the family. "Time for me to go!" he said. "Remember, Tom... one day we'll be running the world!"

That evening Tantrum the cat was found curled up asleep in the laundry basket. Some instinct had told her that she would be able to relax in peace.

Tom missed Mr Hi-Tech, but he was glad to find Mary Pickles at home again when he came back from school.